The Tears of God

BENEDICT J. GROESCHEL, C.F.R.

The Tears of God

Going on in the Face of
Great Sorrow or Catastrophe

IGNATIUS PRESS   SAN FRANCISCO

Cover art: "For God So Loved the World . . ."
© 1999 by Nelson Woodcraft

(For information on this image as well as a full line of hand-crafted, high-quality Catholic religious goods, contact: Nelson Woodcraft, P.O. Box 4515 Steubenville, OH 43952. Telephone 1-800-895-6267. www.nelsonwoodcraft.com)

Cover design by Riz Boncan Marsella

© 2009 Ignatius Press, San Francisco
All rights reserved
ISBN 978-1-58617-289-3
Library of Congress Control Number 2008933492
Printed in the United States of America ∞

I gratefully dedicate this book to all who helped me to survive a catastrophe—being hit by a car on January 11, 2004. I am grateful to God for making it possible for me to think and work and even get around.

This book is an act of gratitude to God and an attempt to help others facing a catastrophe. I wish to thank Father John Lynch and David Burns who were with me and remained with me at the time of the accident. Their presence, no doubt, kept me alive because the attending physicians had given up when I had no vital signs for fifteen minutes. In response to an appeal from Father Lynch, they went on, and after another thirteen minutes, my heart started to beat again.

I will be ever grateful to the doctors, nurses, and staff of Orlando Regional Medical Center, and especially to the trauma team. I am also very grateful for the support I received from my sister Marjule, who remained at my side, and all the friars who came and remained with her and supported her during those difficult weeks. I am also grateful to thousands of people who prayed for me, especially through EWTN, and to the fifty thousand people of many denominations and faiths who sent me e-mails, letters, and cards telling me of their prayers. Whatever one wishes to conclude, prayer is a very effective means of responding to catastrophe.

I wish to thank an anonymous hermit priest, who prepared this manuscript, and Kathie McCusker, who carefully checked the text.

—Fr. Benedict J. Groeschel, C.F.R.
January 11, 2008
Trinity Retreat, Larchmont, N.Y.

Contents

Preface

Faith and Catastrophe

Some time ago, I published the most popular book I ever wrote, *Arise from Darkness*. It is a book about what to do when life doesn't make sense. Many people have told me that it was helpful to them in difficult times with problems of the family, with the Church, with finances, with themselves. I became aware, however, that there was another group of people who read the book but whom I had not reached: those who had suffered catastrophes or horrors. We all have sorrow, but we don't all have the horrible in our lives. But it *does* come. It comes to people we know, and maybe some day it will come to us, and we will have to be prepared.

I had thought of waiting to write a book like this until I was dying of a terminal illness because then I would have a personal experience of the catastrophic. Devastating events of life have happened to me in the past, but nothing that I could call a real catastrophe. Then, I was struck by an automobile and lived through a real catastrophe. It turned out that it was not as bad at it originally seemed, and I have been able, with limitations, to get back to my pastoral work. But it lives on still. As I awoke in the hospital from three weeks of unconsciousness and realized that I could hardly move, I thought, "Well, Benedict, you've had your catastrophe. Get writing."

Many years ago, I read a book that deeply moved me, *Hour of Gold, Hour of Lead*, by Anne Morrow Lindbergh. She pointed out that into all lives comes sorrow but only into some lives comes horror. It had come to her and her husband, Charles, in the form of the kidnapping and murder of their infant son. She tells us in that book that as she tried to recount her horror, her long road back to where the tragedy "is buried is overlaid with new life", and that, undoubtedly "the long road of insight, suffering, healing and rebirth is best illustrated in the Christian religion by the suffering, death and resurrection of Christ."[1]

I am writing this book now, first of all, for those who have experienced horror or catastrophe in their lives. This includes the appreciable number of people that you read about in the course of a month in the newspapers of any city. Not only are there murders and accidents and firefighters or police killed in the line of duty, there is often the terrible news of young men and women being killed in military service. As I write this, we are involved in the conflict in Iraq, which frequently brings accounts of the deaths of many innocent people on all sides. Not only this, but we read about natural disasters ranging from tornadoes to the collapse of bridges. We read about unspeakable tragedies in families where sometimes a family member, apparently out of the blue, kills other members of the family or innocent children, or a neighbor loses his mind and goes on a rampage, as happened in the case of the girls in the Amish schoolhouse in 2006.

[1] Anne Morrow Lindbergh, *Hour of Gold, Hour of Lead* (New York: Harcourt Brace Jovanovich, 1973), pp. 213–14.

These are all horrors and catastrophes. Add to them the death of small children, whose terminal illnesses are catastrophic. The death of an older person, although it may leave many people deeply saddened, is not usually considered a catastrophe; when the person is the mother or father of small children, however, it deserves that designation. Personal moral failures or false accusations often bring catastrophic consequences, which are generally not described as horrors.

This book is written especially for those who are in this category, who are experiencing or have recently experienced horror or catastrophe.

It is also written for those who are closely related to those who have experienced catastrophe—family and close friends. These are people who are deeply affected, but not directly damaged by the catastrophe. They are there to help. They participate by sympathy and empathy in each phase of the problem, and their own lives are often changed almost as much as those who have been the victims.

Third, this book is for those who are aware of catastrophes around them, who read about them in the newspaper and pause to say a prayer, who think about those who have been deeply hurt and realize that such things could happen to them. Not long before the writing of this book, a beautiful family was killed by criminal desperados who broke into their home and left only one parent alive. Day after day, I remembered this family in my prayers, and although I never met them, I suffered with them. Don't we often think of such things as we pass through life? And each one of us who is thoughtful and reflective knows that such a thing could happen to us. We pray to God that it doesn't, but it is wise to meditate on the possibility and to think about what you would do and where you would turn. This book is also written for this group of people.

A Book about Faith

It is rather obvious, considering the authorship of this book, that it is about faith, faith in God and, further, faith in a God who cares about us when we are in need. But by catastrophe, faith can be severely tried, and it may even lead to questioning. Faith in God has often, in the past, particularly in the Bible, been put to great trial. Over and over again the psalmist in the Jewish Scriptures asks God: "Where are You? Why did You let this happen? How long are You going to let it go on?"

Psalm 88

Lord my God, I call for help by day;
I cry at night before you.
Let my prayer come into your presence.
O turn your ear to my cry.

For my soul is filled with evils;
my life is on the brink of the grave,
I am reckoned as one in the tomb:
I have reached the end of my strength,

like one alone among the dead;
like the slain lying in their graves;
like those you remember no more,
cut off, as they are from your hand.

You have laid me in the depths of the tomb,
in places that are dark, in the depths.
Your anger weighs down upon me:
I am drowned beneath your waves. . . .

As for me, Lord, I call to you for help:
in the morning my prayer comes before you.
Lord, why do you reject me?
Why do you hide your face?

Wretched, close to death from my youth,
I have borne my trials; I am numb.[2]

In the Christian Gospels, we have the example of the Son of God Himself weeping at the death of His friend Lazarus, and particularly asking His Father on the Cross, "Why have you forsaken me?" These two events gave rise to the title of this book, *The Tears of God*. For the Christian, the tears of Jesus of Nazareth are the tears of God. The only way that the Divine Being could enter into the sufferings of mankind was to take on a true human body and soul. That is the mystery of the Word made flesh.

If you are reading this book at a time of personal tragedy, you may even be inclined to be cynical about

[2] Translation from the Hebrew (© 1963 by The Grail, England). Adapted for the *Liturgy of the Hours* (London: Collins, 1974).

or angry at God. May I ask you to keep reading? This reaction, while not the best, is totally understandable and one that apparently Christ Himself in some way faced in His life. The cry from the Cross, "Why have you abandoned me?" expresses a feeling that, like a cold chill, can come over a fervent believer. But we must go on. Part of the answer for us is to look more deeply into what Christ and His followers have suffered during their lives and to come to some understanding that God uses catastrophe ultimately as part of the great work of salvation, for the human race and for the individual.

Recently, a slate of atheistic writers, vitriolic in their hostility to religion, have used tragedy or the problem of evil to attack the idea of the providence of God. In this book, we will not try to answer them because their general approach has been so hostile and lacking in objectivity that it would be useless to respond to them. But, to respond to the question "Why?" that echoes in so many human hearts, we will try to give some reasonable answers, which may not be thoroughly satisfying, but which may be a help in a time of tragedy and catastrophe.

CHAPTER ONE

Tragedies and Catastrophes
Happen All the Time

Anyone living in a fairly large metropolitan area is aware that the newspapers at least every other day include the description of some personal tragedy or even larger-scale catastrophe. It is strange that we can read accounts of these events and remain almost totally unmoved, or perhaps just experience a tinge of sympathy. The headline shouts out, "FIREFIGHTER KILLED IN COLLAPSING BUILDING!" If you are devout, you may pause for a moment to say a prayer for the firefighter and his family and look with compassion on the photograph of his wife and children leaving the funeral. You cannot do more than that in a big city because you would be preoccupied all the time with tragedies. Those who live in less-congested areas may only hear of a disaster once a week or even perhaps a bit less often. But tragedies are all around us, and it is important to realize that this dark thread runs through the fabric of all human life.

The larger catastrophes of the human race we come to accept as news events unless they happen to us or near us. I recall being on pilgrimage in Assisi and being told by an old Italian friar that a catastrophe had happened in New York. I ran into the retreat house of the Graymoor Sisters and saw the television on, with the sisters gathered tearfully around. There were indescribable pictures of the World Trade Center Towers cascading down. It was so unreal that for the moment, I didn't ask myself the question: How many people were inside?

In a few minutes, it began to dawn on me that there would be many casualties. When I got home as quickly as possible, I learned that over three thousand people had been killed. A number of those killed were friends of mine or members of the families of friends of mine. One priest friend had thirty-two funerals in his parish for people who had died in the World Trade Center. This single attack was an almost incomprehensible catastrophe.

The Archdiocese of New York kept two priests down at the morgue center in the midst of the ruins for several weeks. We all volunteered to spend eight hours there praying as crews brought in the human remains that they had found. Often this was only a small plastic bag. We all prayed together, and a very professional lady, called a forensic anthropologist, would identify the kind of person to whom this particular set of remains had belonged —a middle-aged woman, an older man. We had learned to live with horror, but each time this happened my mind turned to the families, some of whom I knew, who had to face this appalling horror. Why had it not happened to me?

Also, most of my readers have lived through significant parts of the twentieth century, a century of war and holocausts. I have known a number of Jewish people who lost a significant portion of their families to the Nazi gas chambers. Some of these people, who are grieving for the rest of their lives, are very close friends of mine. I became accustomed on the anniversary of the so-called Crystal Night to visit Jewish families who had lost relatives to the Nazis fifty years before. What struck me was their ability to go on, their ability to live through the memory of such a horrible catastrophe.

Besides my Jewish friends, I also heard firsthand accounts from some Capuchin friars from Krakow, to whom I had the opportunity to teach English. Most of them had been prisoners four and a half years at the Dachau concentration camp. One large friary of over thirty men had been arrested on a single day. Only seven survived, and they had incredible memories of the cruelty and horror that had lasted nearly five years.

One particularly brave priest, Monsignor Arthur Rojeck, a pastor in the New York Archdiocese, had been a prisoner four and a half years. Strangely, he had been saved from death by an S.S. soldier who intervened and kept him from being injected with air into his veins, and who had, as gently as possible, cut off his infected finger and sewed it up. Monsignor Rojeck did not like to dwell on what had happened to him, but he lived all his life in the shadow of those horrible years. Strangely, and this is insightful, he said, "I cannot now wish that it had not happened because those years made me who I am today." This is often what happens to a person who survives catastrophe.

From this brief discussion of the catastrophes that surround us, including the catastrophic death of small children, the onset of severe insanity, the coming of progressive, and eventually fatal, diseases like ALS (Lou Gehrig's disease)—in the midst of all of this, compassionate people must feel that they should take some part in others' grief. To pass from life in this world without an attitude of compassion and concern for the catastrophes of others is probably one of the worst possible states that a person can occupy. Christ's words in the Gospel of Saint Luke, "Woe to you that laugh now, for you shall weep" (6:25), seem to be aimed at those who are surrounded by others' sufferings and sorrows but manage simply to avoid any involvement. That's a catastrophe all its own.

> No man is an island, entire of itself;
> every man is a piece of the continent,
> a part of the main.
>
> —John Donne

The words of this well-known poet remind us all that we are part of the human race, which, although surrounded by many blessings and many good things, nonetheless, constantly faces catastrophe and sorrow. If you are in the midst of your own personal tragedy as you read this book, keep in mind that you have plenty of company. Remember that all around us, perhaps on the next block or at least in the next town, there are people going through similar sorrows. You are not alone. One of the conclusions of this book is that we grow when we ex-perience catastrophe by becoming more sympathetic and concerned about other people. The only other alternative is to turn inwardly into our own imaginary sanctuary and there to live in isolated and narcissistic self-indulgence. That, perhaps, is the greatest catastrophe of them all, but it will only be recognized at the end of life.

CHAPTER TWO

The Catastrophes That Happen

It seemed to me, as I was writing this book, that it would be helpful to outline the different kinds of catastrophes. If you are suffering through a catastrophe, you might just skim through the sections that don't pertain to you. If, on the other hand, you are reading because you want to prepare yourself for the possibility of catastrophe or to understand how to help others caught in great difficulties and sorrow, it would be wise to consider carefully the different kinds of misfortunes that may occur.

As we prepare to do this, it is important to keep in mind that we are created by the all-powerful God to have joy and complete fulfillment. That is what awaits us after the end of this difficult life. Men are enmeshed in what is called "the problem of evil". Sacred Scripture gives, in a very simple way, the origin of the evils that beset men, descendants of the first parents called Adam and Eve. Why this evil comes down upon us all is completely mysterious.

Having written about sorrow and difficulty before, I have spent a good deal of time pondering the mystery of evil. Saint Thomas Aquinas remarks that the problem of evil is why most people who don't believe, don't believe, and why most people who do believe, do believe. Evil

appears to have no answer at all if you do not believe in
God and to be very puzzling even if you do.

It seems to me that Christians concentrating on the
infinite power and goodness of God often miss the fact
that human life is a great battle, as Saint Thomas calls it,
"a strange duel between good and evil". If you wonder
how powerful evil can be, just think of the holocausts,
wars, revolutions and devastations of the twentieth century. Incredible evil is possible everywhere. Evil comes
to a white-hot point in the life of Christ when He is led
to His terrible Passion and death. Our Lord, in the so-
liloquy that precedes the Passion narrative in the Gospel
of Saint John, makes it clear that His coming Passion is
the work of Satan and that the ruler of this world will be
overcome by His death. After a voice from the heavens
responds, proclaiming that God will glorify His name,
Christ says: " 'This voice has come for your sake, not for
mine. Now is the judgment of this world, now shall the
ruler of this world be cast out; and I, when I am lifted
up from the earth, will draw all men to myself.' He said
this to show by what death he was to die" (Jn 12:30–33).
The teaching of the conflict between good and evil in the
Passion is one that is sometimes overlooked, even though
the reason given for the Passion is that Satan entered into
the heart of Judas Iscariot (Jn 13:27).

We should realize deep within ourselves that there is
a conflict going on in this world mirroring the conflict
between good and evil that took place in the ages beyond
time. This conflict is recalled in the Book of Revelation

when it says, "war broke out in heaven" (12:7, NAB). We tend to avoid reading the Book of Revelation, or at least applying it to our own times, because it is so mysterious. However, if one takes an honest look at what goes on in human life and history, one sees that the great conflicts between good and evil, between the angels of God and Satan in the Book of Revelation, ring very true. This, despite the fact that the Book of Revelation is filled with mystery, should give us comfort.

People often ask the question: "If God made everything perfect, why did He make an imperfect world?" This is not a silly question. And part of the answer is shrouded in mystery. The most obvious answer is that by patient endurance and by faith and trust, even in darkness, we become prepared for our salvation. We don't earn it because it has been earned by Christ, but by being His disciples and carrying the cross, as He said we must, we become worthy of being called His disciples and entering into the Kingdom of God. No one reading the Gospels or any part of the New Testament can have a doubt that the disciples of Christ must suffer with Him.[1]

The general assumption of paleontologists and archeologists is that the human race began in Africa in what is now Kenya; if not there, then in the Near East. If you

---

[1] Because of the importance of this question, I spent some time working on it in a book called *Healing the Original Wound* (Ann Arbor, Mich.: Servant Publications, 1993). The reader interested in the question of Original Sin, good and evil, salvation and redemption might find that book helpful at this time.

were to go to Africa now, you would find immense numbers of children left without parents because of the catastrophic epidemic of AIDS. When one thinks that each of these orphaned children has a human life and feelings of his own, that each one of them lives out life with the needs for happiness and some comfort that all men have, the question shrieks out to you, "Why?" What did these orphan children ever do to deserve being brought into the world and losing their parents to this terrible illness? This is one of ten thousand examples I could give of the problem of evil. Unfortunately, in Western civilization it has become commonplace for people to insulate themselves from evil, not to look beyond the headlines. Evil is a mystery, and we must recognize it as mysterious. This is not difficult to do when we consider the beauty and order of human life, the marvelous potentials of men and then we see the devastating effects of evil. It's a mystery.

Presently, many people have difficulty dealing with the concept of the mysterious. They believe, especially if they are religious people, that everything should be understandable and reasonable. This, it turns out, is a popular misconception of our time. Immense numbers of things that come under the scope of science are completely mysterious, things like gravity, time, life itself. Many aspects of the human personality are mysterious—why we wish to do one thing and end up doing something else, why we are mysteries to ourselves.

Life itself is mysterious, and those who fail to come to grips with mystery either are very naïve or very angry or end up being both. Many of the attacks on religion, which as we mentioned, are in the popular press at the present time, are ultimately based on a refusal to come to grips with mystery. The greatest scientist who ever lived, Albert Einstein, had this to say about mystery:

> The most beautiful and most profound emotion we can experience is the sensation of the mystical. It is the sower of all true science. He to whom this emotion is a stranger, who can no longer wonder and stand rapt in awe, is as good as dead. To know what is impenetrable to us really exists, manifesting itself as the highest wisdom and the most radiant beauty which our dull faculties can comprehend only in their most primitive forms—this knowledge, this feeling is at the center of true religiousness.
>
> My religion consists of a humble admiration of the illimitable superior spirit who reveals himself in the slight details we are able to perceive with our frail and feeble minds. That deeply emotional conviction of the presence of a superior reasoning power, which is revealed in the incomprehensible universe, forms my idea of God.[2]

Physical Ills

The most common kind of evils and disasters that may occur to a person are the following: physical illnesses, accidents, inherited genetic disorders, epidemics, and things like this. We sometimes, in the make-believe safety of our more scientifically advanced culture, think that we are immune from these things. Nonetheless, epidemics

[2] Lincoln Barnett. *The Universe and Dr. Einstein*, with introduction by Albert Einstein (New York: William Morrow and Company, 1948), p. 105.

like AIDS do occur, and we are warned by scientists that there may be a great epidemic called a pandemic. Apart from these, there are ordinary ills and fatal illnesses that men may face. A person in apparently good health, who has been mindful of health, may suddenly, while jogging, drop dead of a heart attack. The person who has fought off serious illness for many years of life may sometimes fall prey to an accident. One should be aware that the possibility of serious physical illness or a severe accident is never far away from any of us. I saw the course of my life change dramatically in a moment's mistake when I looked the wrong way and stepped into oncoming traffic.

Natural Disasters

Most people go through life thinking that they will avoid a natural disaster. However, something as simple as lightning striking a house or a defective electric wire may plunge us into the worst of disasters. We often hear reports of floods, tornadoes, hurricanes, forest fires in different parts of the world. There seems to be no part of the world that is completely free of the possibility of natural disasters, although some places are obviously safer than others. Not too long ago, we were all appalled by a tidal wave, or tsunami, striking along the coasts of India and Indonesia. It was utterly unexpected, caused by an undersea earthquake. My office is just a few feet from the seawall of a bay on Long Island Sound. It seems like a very quiet place, but a few years ago one of my neighbors was washed away in the waves from a hurricane. Natural disasters are always a possibility.

Evil Purposely Done

The history of the world is filled with people doing evil deeds to others. Some were done by those with evil intentions who thrust their own destructive impulses on others. But often evil is done by people who think that they are doing good. Many of the most dangerous political ideologies in the twentieth century were led by people who thought they were benefiting the human race. One has only to think of the victims of Bolshevik Communism, Nazism, and, more recently, Muslim extremism to realize that evils done on purpose for what people wrongly believe is a good cause lead to a tremendous amount of suffering and catastrophe. Hitler, Stalin, and Mao all thought they were great benefactors of mankind. In their paranoia and pride, they brutally extinguished the lives of millions.

Along with this spectacular kind of evil is simply crime, evil committed against another person for one's own good or satisfaction. Often, in the case of criminals, it's possible to trace how these people were put on this destructive road by their childhood experiences. Having worked for many years as chaplain of an agency seeking to assist disturbed and delinquent youngsters, many of whom had been exposed to crime and physical abuse, I understand how a youngster can grow into an adult who does monstrous deeds. What about the victims of all of these things —the victims' families destroyed by some criminal act or some act of insanity, their children harmed or abused or destroyed? How does one account for this evil, when evil is done by those who have volunteered to be helpers of mankind, including members of the clergy? This is all the more appalling. It becomes a catastrophe, and even a horror, although the person perpetrating these deeds may never have started out in life with any intention to harm another.

Personal Evil

Any of us honestly looking into our own personalities can see selfish and even possibly destructive elements there. We would not like to look at these dynamics, but often, in psychotherapy, they come up to the surface. It is unwise even to think that such evil is not possible for oneself. Consider the men whom Jesus called to be His closest supporters and followers. They lived with Him for three years. They saw His miracles, heard His blessed teaching, and yet, because of fear and weakness, they deserted Him at the time He needed them the most, and one of them actually betrayed and sold Him. The catastrophe of personal evil is always a possibility.

Communal Evil

At times, whole societies are foolishly or wickedly pulled into incredibly evil behavior. Often this is done by people of good will intending to do good things. One has only to think of the death of tens of millions of innocent children in the United States and many other countries through abortion. Those who support and pursue this murderous procedure often are very civilized and consciously well-intentioned people. They are deceived about the nature of what they are doing, and it would be appropriate to say that they are deceived by the evil one, as were the leaders of the political ideologies listed above. Think of the immense evil done to the United States by abortion and visited upon it by men who were carefully chosen to be just judges.

Another great evil in the United States, which unfortunately and strangely is not spoken of very often, was the treatment of African people who were brought here as slaves. The slavery that existed in the United States was of an atrocious kind unparalleled in modern times. The Supreme Court of the United States in 1857, in the case of Dred Scott, a runaway slave, declared that he was only chattel, an object like a piece of furniture; that he had no rights at all. This terrible judgment of the Supreme Court precipitated the Civil War. It's interesting that the chief justice and some other justices who made this decision themselves personally thought that slavery was wrong, but they voted for a compromise.

Even after the Emancipation Proclamation, the treatment of African Americans remained atrocious. Severe laws were enacted, especially in the Southern part of the United States, forcing them into a situation of extreme poverty and humiliation. Even in the North, there was a great deal of segregation and injustice that lasted right up until the 1960s. It was, in fact, an inspired Protestant minister, Martin Luther King Jr., who led the mobilization of African Americans and other Americans against this evil of segregation and abuse. The situation of African-American people has changed considerably since that time, but there are still the remnants and ghosts of that terrible injustice around. This can be seen if you visit a county jail practically anywhere. There are a disproportionate number of inmates who are African-American. This is because they grew up with lack of opportunity and a feeling of being inferior. This evil, like abortion, continues today. It is the darkest page in American history.[3]

A more recent evil has been the abuse of undocumented workers. Millions of undocumented workers have been accepted into the United States by the open cooperation and connivance of our civil government. They were allowed to come in because no one else would do the back-breaking work that they do for such small wages. Many leaders in agriculture and food production will admit that they could not go on without these workers, and yet, suddenly by draconian laws, undocumented workers have been put in a situation where they cannot legally earn

---

[3] The African-American experience, mysteriously enough, also brought out great spiritual beauty. "Where sin abounded, grace did more abound." While people were being treated unjustly and horribly, they generated their own spirituality with hymns and prayers. We do not pay enough attention to the simple Bible spirituality worked out by the African-American people in the face of a terrible evil and injustice.

their daily bread. It's impossible to move a population of nine or ten million working people in a month's time, and so what is done is that they are forced into a position of being violators of law, and so are their employers. Since the law is unenforceable in the case of such large numbers, we have invited law enforcement agents to select those whom they wish to punish or get even with, for entirely personal reasons. We open the country to widespread bribery and manipulation of public officials by unrealistic laws that can't be equally applied. Employers will be forced to bribe or to befriend political leaders and police in order to keep from being selected as the representatives of employers of undocumented people. On top of this is the fact that all of these workers contribute six percent of their salary to Social Security and will never collect a penny of that money. This injustice, totaling billions of dollars every year, is what the Old Testament refers to as a sin that cries to heaven for punishment.

We are all involved in evil. It's impossible to live in this world without becoming unwillingly involved in some injustice or evil. But our discussion is not about ourselves but rather about those who are the victims of evil. All of the people we have listed above—from those who are seriously hurt by reckless drivers to aborted unborn children to people imprisoned and even unjustly executed when someone else is guilty—all of these are victims of catastrophic evils and horrors that occur in daily life because of injustice.

People are uncomfortable when religion, especially the Bible, speaks about the judgment of God. They would like to have a picture of God, who, because He is infinitely good, sees everything as pleasant and amusing. This is not true. In order to right the wrongs of the world, in order to reestablish divine justice, to make good triumph over evil, the Eternal Word of God, equal to the Father in all things, came and took upon Himself a true human body and a true human soul in the womb of the Virgin Mary. He lived a poor life of hard work, deprivation, and ultimate misunderstanding. He died under the most painful torture imaginable, and He did this so that evil would be overcome by good. This is something that, when we are in the grips of evil being done against us, whether on purpose or not, we should remember: God Himself in the person of His Son endured the evils that mysteriously haunt human life on earth.

It might be well to recall that Christians belong to the only religion in the world that believes in a God who suffers, a God who dies.

CHAPTER THREE

Evil That Does Not Become the Worst

Saint Augustine taught that God does not cause evil but causes that evil does not become the worst. A person in the midst of the struggle with a catastrophe or a horror is not likely to remember this. But, in fact, the worst of evils comes to an end and even, possibly, brings forth good results. The famous saying "God writes straight with crooked lines" can even be emphasized to the point of saying, "God writes very straight with very crooked lines."

One of the most significant signs of Divine Providence is how, if one continues on with faith, even the worst and most dreadful of catastrophes may, in the long run, lead to good or, at least, be replaced by another good.

For example, my old Jewish friends escaped from the Nazis and eventually found peaceful and comfortable lives in America. They were drawn together in friendship and support of each other. The anniversary of the "Crystal Night" (when the worst pogroms began in Germany) brought a group of them together in one of the most unique and moving times of human sharing I have ever witnessed, although it appeared only to be a dinner shared by a group of elderly people.

One of my friends, whose children were killed, has spent a quiet life doing good works, going on so bravely that most people she helps have no idea of the hell she came through.

It is worth recalling that anticipated catastrophes often don't happen at all or are brought to unforeseeable conclusions. In the case of illness, this may even be what medical doctors will identify as "a miracle". I myself am an example of such a thing. I went twenty-seven minutes with no vital signs at all, including no blood pressure, heartbeat, or respiration. The excellent and dedicated physicians and nurses attending me in the Orlando Trauma Center were rightly about to give up when Father John Lynch, who was with me, begged them to go on. They assured him that there was no hope, and if I did survive, I would be in a "vegetative" state. The actual fact is that, despite all serious predictions, I am able to function, think, and with some difficulty, even walk. I am, in fact, busier than I have ever been in my life. Here was a catastrophe that did not play itself out. Interestingly, I'm a medical miracle but not a miracle for the Catholic Church, which requires that the cure be instant and complete.

There are also serious diseases that don't take their predicted course. There are people who recover, as I did, from extremely alarming medical conditions.

Sometimes these recoveries take place in a very obvious religious circumstance like the cure of a person at a shrine. Dr. Alexis Carrel, a Nobel Prize winner in medicine, has left a description of watching one of these miracles occur. At the end, when the woman came back to life with no symptoms of tuberculosis, he wrote, "I have seen the resurrection of the dead."[1]

Often people survive incredible hardship and deadly situations, and there is no explanation. Practically every older person who has been in touch with people from Europe during the Second World War has met someone who survived the concentration camps and who managed to escape or to survive until the Allies arrived. Sometimes there is absolutely no human explanation for this.

The brave Russian writer, Aleksandr Solzhenitsyn, took on the Soviet Union and the Communist government directly in his writings while still living there. Such brave behavior and outspokenness had brought millions of people to immediate execution or condemnation to the gradual death of the mines in Siberia. In some remarkable way, Solzhenitsyn survived and has been one of the great witnesses against totalitarianism in our time. Look into your memory and just think of the people you know who are alive despite similar near-death experiences. I know two men who survived the invasions at Normandy and at Anzio and were in the midst of the bloodshed when practically every person with them had been killed. One of these, a Capuchin friar, Father Bruno, actually walked upright around the beach expecting to be killed at any

---

[1] Alexis Carrel, *The Voyage to Lourdes* (Frazer, Mich.: Real-View Books, 1994), cited in Fr. Benedict Groeschel, *The Journey toward God* (Ann Arbor, Mich.: Servant Publications, 2000).

moment while giving the sacrament of holy anointing to the dying soldiers. For some reason, he was never even wounded.

The questions may occur to any reader who has been through a catastrophe: "Why did this good outcome not happen to me? Was God not watching over me?" Or "Is a good outcome in a bad situation simply a matter of chance?" These are very legitimate questions addressed in the next chapter. It is, however, obvious that there are people who should certainly have had catastrophic results from what happened to them, and, somehow, they did not.

Part of the answer may simply include a willingness to go on. I have heard it said by concentration camp victims of both the Nazis and the Bolsheviks that those prisoners who wanted to live had the best chance of surviving. Many became so despondent in their circumstances that they did not make the necessary adjustments to survive. Hope, even on a purely human level, can be a factor in survival.

The consequences of disaster are often determined by the victim's decision to manage with what was left to him. We all know people who went on bravely to lead new lives. I know a few people who saw horrible mishaps like their children being taken away by acts of violence or catastrophe who went on. An acquaintance, who lost his whole family in a terrible boating accident, raised a second family of his own.

An idea that can be very helpful in any catastrophe is

that "all things are passing" to use the words of Saint Teresa of Avila. In the worst of situations, especially if trouble has come on very suddenly, it may be impossible "to get your arms around this idea". However when the initial shock subsides and the long period of desperation begins, it is wise to recall that each day brings a step away from the trouble.

It is immensely beneficial at this time if one can pray and even make an act of faith and hope. Often at least the beginning of forgiveness is even more helpful. Immaculée Ilibagiza found the grace to go and help many thousands after the suffering during the Rwandan holocaust, which she recounts in her testimony, *Left to Tell*. Her family had all been killed.

> We carried the bodies of my mother and my brother into the ruins of our home and dug a large grave in the center of one of the rooms where laughter and love once had echoed. There were no priests left in the village, so we performed the burial rites ourselves. We said some of my mother's favorite hymns and prayed many prayers. I asked God to hold my family close to Him and watch over their beautiful souls in heaven . . . and then I said good-bye.
>
> Soon we were in the clouds again, flying high above my village, high above the sorrow that had stained our lives . . . so high that I felt I could touch the face of God.[2]

When I interviewed Immaculée on my program I could hardly imagine what horrors she had survived, but she

[2] Immaculée Ilibagiza with Steve Erwin, *Left to Tell* (Carlsbad, Calif.: Hay House, 2006).

goes on with faith, hope and forgiveness. She proves Saint Augustine's teaching that God keeps evil from becoming the worst.

Immaculée's prayer for her brutally murdered family brings us another insight especially helpful in the case of terminal illness—that is, the transitory or pasting nature of human life. All that we have and experience, the good and the bad, will come to an end. Christ admonishes us in the Gospel account of the tower that collapsed in Siloam, killing eighteen people. He tells us that those who perished were no worse that anybody else but we should bear in mind that we should avoid sin and do good or we will have a worse fate (Lk 13:4–5).

CHAPTER FOUR

When the Storm Goes By

When the immediate encounter with a catastrophe or horror has passed and one is left simply with the effects, which may be extremely painful, what should one do? One must first expect a period of disorientation. This is particularly true after an accident or some other unforeseen disastrous event like a house burning down or someone being killed or seriously injured or even being arrested. There is a time of grief, disorientation, and trying to "pick up the pieces". In the midst of all this, there are usually friends and others coming to the rescue, trying to be helpful, to listen, to make suggestions. At times, one may even get impatient with their suggestions because they often will be rather obvious. No one really knows exactly what to do.

People of faith, at this point, must embrace their belief in God. There's no way around this. We are reassured by the Old Testament and the New Testament that Divine Providence cares for those who trust in God. The famous lines from the Twenty-third Psalm bring this out so clearly:

Even though I walk through the valley of the shadow
of death,

> I fear no evil;
>   for you are with me;
> your rod and your staff,
>   they comfort me.
> You prepare a table before me
>   in the presence of my enemies. . . .
> Surely goodness and mercy shall follow me
>   all the days of my life.

This is one of an immense number of quotations in the Old Testament stating that we must place our trust in God. They coexist with many other statements where the person praying questions why God has not helped him, and cries out to God in desperation.

> My God, my God, why have you forsaken me?
> You are far from my plea and the cry of my distress.
> O my God, I call by day and you give no reply;
> I call by night and I find no peace.
>
> (Ps 22:2−3) [1]

The words of this psalm are identical to the words spoken by Jesus on the cross. In fact, some of the Fathers of the Church believe that our Lord recited the entire psalm while He was on the Cross. The words of this psalm contrast with such reassuring statements of Jesus as "Ask, and you will receive. Seek, and you will find. Knock, and it will be opened to you" (Mt 7:7, NAB). Saint Paul goes so far as to say that for those who trust God, all things work together unto good (Rom 8:28).

---

[1] *The Liturgy of the Hours*, Psalms texts © The Grail (London: Collins, 1963).

People of faith must struggle to bring their catastrophes or even horrors into some kind of relationship with these reassurances of God's love. The mysterious fact is that dreadful things can happen to the person who has trust in God. Often, as we have seen, there are examples of dreadful things that did not happen, like people surviving and coming back home from horrible concentration camps and people recovering from incredible illnesses or accidents. But, on the other hand, there are those who do not survive, do not recover. The question comes, "Is God playing games with us?"

This is where a person of faith must adopt a broad vision. The purpose of this life is not to bring to us permanent happiness here on earth. Some happiness comes along the way, it is true. It often comes unexpectedly to many people. One can meet those who are born with catastrophic illnesses and are often rather happy and contented people, just as one can meet a few who enjoy good health and a very prosperous life, and who, at the same time, manage to be quite unhappy.

The question is *What do we see as the purpose of life?* For the Christian believer, the purpose of life must be seen as the entrance into eternal life.

> "Let not your hearts be troubled; believe in God, believe also in me. In my Father's house are many rooms; if it were not so, would I have told you that I go to prepare a place for you? And when I go and prepare a place for you, I will come again and will take you to myself, that where I am you may be also. And you know the way where I am going." Thomas said to him, "Lord, we do not know

where you are going; how can we know the way?" Jesus said to him, "I am the way, and the truth, and the life; no one comes to the Father, but by me" (Jn 14:1–6).

If we strive to do so, whatever else happens, we will be brought to eternal life. Saint Paul is one of the New Testament writers who is most emphatic about this and often proclaims that, in the midst of great need and suffering, he knows that God is leading him on the way.

> For I think that God has exhibited us apostles as last of all, like men sentenced to death; because we have become a spectacle to the world, to angels and to men. We are fools for Christ's sake, but you are wise in Christ. We are weak, but you are strong. You are held in honor, but we in disrepute. To the present hour we hunger and thirst, we are ill-clad and buffeted and homeless, and we labor, working with our own hands. When reviled, we bless; when persecuted, we endure; when slandered, we try to conciliate; we have become, and are now, as the refuse of the world, the offscouring of all things (1 Cor 4:9–13).

Despite all of this and Saint Paul's dramatic expression, repeated more than once, of the difficulties of the apostles and of himself, we witness an entirely different sentiment in another quotation. This is a statement of complete trust in God: "For I am sure that neither death, nor life, nor angels, nor principalities, nor things present, nor things to come, nor powers, nor height, nor depth, nor anything else in all creation, will be able to separate us from the love of God in Christ Jesus our Lord" (Rom 8:38–39).

The believer must go on with the clear conviction, even in the midst of horror, that God will bring this all to good in eternal life. If we think of the immense number of people who died in concentration camps during the Second World War, and later under Stalin, we realize that many of them died cherishing this hope. Often scratched into the walls of the camps are crosses, Scripture quotations, and words indicating eternal hope on the part of those who faced torture and death. The example of Saint Maximilian Kolbe, in the face of monstrous evil, stands out. This priest, who had been extremely effective and a fervent apostle, having established the largest monastery of friars in the world, was condemned to Auschwitz, vilified, beaten, and left for dead. When the man next to him was singled out to be starved to death as a hostage, Kolbe asked to take his place and was permitted to do so. His life and death are incredible examples of hope. His generosity spared another human being, a man I met in his old age, who had spent his life giving testimony to the courage and incredible charity of Saint Maximilian.

It could be said that, down through the ages, the martyrs have challenged the worst of evil and have won. There is a saying that the martyr begins his work the day that he dies. Of course a person must have belief in eternal life, in the world to come, in the last judgment in order to accept this promise. This is where faith comes and shows us the way in the midst of horror and evil.

God Knows Best

This simple statement was a very popular saying, particularly for Irish people during the long years of struggle and poverty they endured as a punishment for being Catholics in their own country. Often in my own youth, when something tragic or sad had happened, I heard Irish people say these words: "God knows best." They are words of simple faith and courage, and they carry a person through. A more sophisticated person may choose to argue with the statement. Arguing with those who are uncomfortable with this idea will not do much good. This simple statement of faith, which is not contained literally in Sacred Scripture, is a response of the believer to the truths of the Scriptures and the Christian faith and tradition.

Weak Faith

What about people of weak faith? They would like to believe. They would like to trust, but they don't feel or experience that their trust in God is strong enough to sustain them through the catastrophe in which they find themselves. This is a difficult situation. Here an individual is caught between two apparent certitudes. One is the truth that God does know best and in the worst of circumstances is leading us onward. The other certitude is complete atheism: That there is nothing and that life has no meaning. I am, by no means, insensitive to the person like this because many people in this age of worldliness and materialism have a kind of weak faith that is not much more than positive opinion or a hunch. This person needs calmly and quietly to sit down and read the Gospel, particularly the Gospel accounts of the Passion of Christ.

It seems that many authors say that the Christian solution to the mystery of evil is meditating on the fact that the Son of God embraced voluntarily the worst evil that men could experience. It is necessary to read these accounts and to meditate on what happened to the best person who ever lived, the person who was most kind and wise, and who came explicitly by His own words "to save the world". I suggest that you carefully read these texts before you go on.

> Then the soldiers of the governor took Jesus into the praetorium, and they gathered the whole battalion before him. And they stripped him and put a scarlet robe upon him, and plaiting a crown of thorns they put it on his head, and put a reed in his right hand. And kneeling before him they mocked him, saying, "Hail, King of the Jews!" And they spat upon him, and took the reed and struck him on the head. And when they had mocked him, they stripped him of the robe, and put his own clothes on him, and led him away to crucify him (Mt 27:27–31).

> And when the sixth hour had come, there was darkness over the whole land until the ninth hour. And at the ninth hour Jesus cried with a loud voice, "Elo-i, Elo-i, lama sabach-thani?" which means, "My God, my God, why hast thou forsaken me?" (Mk 15:33–34).

> Two others also, who were criminals, were led away to be put to death with him. And when they came to the place which is called The Skull, there they crucified him, and the criminals, one on the right and one on the left. And Jesus said, "Father, forgive them; for they know not what they do." And they cast lots to divide his garments. And the people stood by, watching; but the rulers scoffed at

him, saying, "He saved others; let him save himself, if he is the Christ of God, his Chosen One!" The soldiers also mocked him, coming up and offering him vinegar, and saying, "If you are the King of the Jews, save yourself!" (Lk 23:32–37).

When Jesus saw his mother, and the disciple whom he loved standing near, he said to his mother, "Woman, behold, your son!" Then he said to the disciple, "Behold, your mother!" And from that hour the disciple took her to his own home.

After this Jesus, knowing that all was now finished, said (to fulfil the scripture), "I thirst." A bowl full of vinegar stood there; so they put a sponge full of the vinegar on hyssop and held it to his mouth. When Jesus had received the vinegar, he said, "It is finished"; and he bowed his head and gave up his spirit (Jn 19:26–30).

Faith tells us that Jesus Christ is the Son of God. He tells us this in His own words, which have been given to the Church by the Holy Spirit in the Gospels. The person with weak faith must meditate on these words, even in a desperate situation. The person with strong faith will probably have intuitively turned to the Cross of Christ. But the person of weak faith may not know what this is about. That person should carefully read at least one of the New Testament accounts of the death of Jesus and His Resurrection in order to experience God's answer to the problem of evil. In His own Son, He has suffered the worst of this world's evils, the most terrible of horrors.

By the Cross of Christ, countless numbers of people

have been able to go on through horror and experience the worst, and yet, come out the other side, pick up the pieces, and go on with faith.

An interesting example of this faith and the importance that the appreciation of the Passion of Christ plays in it can be found at Dachau concentration camp. This horrible place was where biological experiments were performed on the prisoners. They were treated as guinea pigs. I know priests who were subjected to these biological experiments by Nazi scientists and who actually survived. One out of every ten people who died in Dachau was a Catholic bishop, priest, brother, or seminarian. In fact, right under the noses of the Dachau guards, a young seminarian dying of tuberculosis was actually ordained a priest.

As one comes into Dachau, which is very precisely preserved, at the back, there is what appears to be a church. The gun tower, or observation tower of the concentration camp, has been made into a steeple. This is our introduction to the Convent of the Holy Blood, cloistered Carmelite nuns who lead lives of prayer and penance in this building, constructed like a barracks of the concentration camp. The altar surmounts what was called "the blood trench" where people were executed.

In front of the convent is a large monument erected by a bishop who was once a prisoner. It is a silo of fieldstone, but with a huge gash or crack in it. Hanging within the silo is a very large metal crown of thorns. This crown of thorns is actually the logo of the present concentration camp, which is kept open as a museum of the Nazi atrocities. Jewish and Protestant monuments are there as well, witnessing to the survival of hope.

When you get into the worst of circumstances you can find that hope is there; not Christians alone, but all people who genuinely believe in a personal God. In the cell in which Saint Maximilian Kolbe was starved to death with nine other men, (and he outlived them all and had to be poisoned,) there now burns continually a beautiful candle marked with the symbols of Easter and a bouquet of flowers—a small, but bright light in the midst of incredible darkness.

We need to know that "we are not among those who draw back and perish, but among those who have faith and live" (Heb 10:39, NAB) and that even weak faith that is mustered and strengthened by prayer, even desperate prayer, can help a person in the midst of great fear, sorrow, and even, horror.

I think that this is what Anne Lindbergh meant when she said that in her days of sorrow and horror at the death of her little child, she found solace in the crucifixion and Resurrection of Christ.

CHAPTER FIVE

Steps of Grief and Sorrow

It usually happens when persons are going through a horrible situation that they can only grasp quickly and intuitively the principles that have become an important part of their lives. A person of faith who has lived by faith will grasp those principles quickly; they will be the only thing they can hold on to. A person with weaker faith, who has perhaps not paid very much attention, will, as we have said, feel disoriented. But this is the moment when they should actually pray. They should call out to God. They should pray by themselves or ask others to pray with them. Even those who don't know how to pray may obtain great benefit by asking someone who is a believer to pray with them. It's a very important thing to do.

However, a person unfamiliar with faith in God, or of little faith, may surprisingly turn to Him in a time of great difficulty and look for those who believe in Him to stand by them. This often happens and requires great gentleness and tact on the part of the convinced believer. It is necessary that the believer is caring but not intrusive and does not argue points of faith that the person in grief may not have come to realize as yet. If you are a believer and you are with someone who is facing a catastrophe,

49

ask them if you can pray with them. They will be confused at the moment, but if you begin to pray in your own words, following the inspirations of the Scriptures, especially of the Lord's Prayer, they may very likely join you, but perhaps silently. Most people know the words of the Lord's Prayer, and it will be something for them to hold on to. Catholics will also, almost intuitively, begin to say the most popular prayer to our Lady, the "Hail Mary". This is a tremendous consolation because Mary went with her Son through the terrible events at the end of His earthly life. People may also want to pray to saints to whom they have felt close and from whom they have experienced assistance. This is, by no means, a bad idea. A saint in heaven may be a familiar and supportive friend to someone in great pain and sorrow.

Once intense prayer is over, it's very important to talk with the persons in grief, to let their grief pour out, to take the time to be there with them, and perhaps even to hold their hands or, if appropriate, to embrace them in some way. In the face of horror or catastrophe, we all regress to a somewhat childlike state. And it is understandable because children need to be held.

In this time when the pansexual theories of the psychoanalytic school are still rather widely, but uncritically, accepted, it is very unfortunate that we see anything like an embrace having some kind of sexual connotation. This thinking has poisoned or stultified many kinds of human relationships. On the one hand, a person has to be careful in such times that he is not misunderstood by an embrace or even by a touch. But at the other times, it may be, in fact, the only way to help a person, particularly in the shock of some terrible experience of death or fear.

When the moment of terror or horror is over, it's very important for the person to "talk it through". I have known extremely brave people who lived through concentration camps who were not inclined to talk it over. Perhaps they had done so when they were first released. Years later, they did not wish to go over the situation. That's understandable. But, having made it a point in life to be friendly and supportive to the victims of concentration camps, both Christians and Jews, I have found that sometimes they still need to talk about it, particularly on the anniversary of something like the Crystal Night when the Nazis broke the windows of all the Jewish businesses and homes they could find in Germany and set fire to many synagogues. An anniversary of this sort is often a time for people to reprocess the horror that they had been through.

Anger at God

A very special consideration must be given to those who are angry at God. A person who has gone through a horror may not be able to explain that anger rationally, but it will be there. I recall a distinguished archbishop of the Armenian Orthodox Church who had himself been born in the wilderness as his family escaped from the Armenian Holocaust in Turkey. He told me that there were people in the Armenian Church from those days who simply could not pray. They remained quietly loyal to the Church. They even attended the liturgy, but they could not pray. I think in such a situation a respectful silence is helpful. Understanding friends should pray for them and with them. Rather than seeing this as a blasphemous anger at God, I would be inclined to see it as emotions that are beyond expression. I would not judge such a person. I have never gone through anything like what they endured. Some spiritual directors even counsel people who are badly hurt "to pray their anger to God".

The Courage of Faith

Faith gives courage, and strong faith gives great courage. Recently, I was deeply moved by the tragedy of a family in which most of the members died at the hands of what must be called "diabolically motivated murderers". I am told that at the funeral service, the father, the only survivor, said: "We must go on with faith. Life must go on." I have heard other people express such feelings in their lives. One young woman I know who found the dead body of her young son, believed to have been killed by a youthful prankster, said to me, "I once read in a book that if you saw all the crosses of the world piled up, you would take the one you have already. I would never have taken this cross. I would rather be dead myself. But since I have been given it to carry, I will carry it." And so she did. This is the courage born of faith.

We need to realize that courage is three distinct things. First, there is a natural quality or virtue that some people have in larger measure than others, which is called courage. *Natural courage* is the ability to face danger (valor) or to endure hardship and continue to do good over a long period of time (perseverance). Then, there is *supernatural courage*, which allows us to face dangers or do difficult things for the sake of the Kingdom of God. Whereas natural courage is expended to lead a decent, good life on earth, supernatural courage points on to eternity. Both kinds of courage may easily exist at the same time and be observed in the same situation.

And thirdly, there is the *gift of courage*, also called fortitude, which is something different. This has been recognized by mystics and theologians over the ages as a special gift of the Holy Spirit. This gift "can pick us up on eagle wings" and give us the ability to do what we would never do on our own, to endure the unendurable, to face the incomprehensible, to go on beyond all normal endurance. This is a gift of God directly, and something that a person cannot in any way acquire themselves. It may be that in the midst of a terrible catastrophe or horror, a person praying humbly but desperately for the gift of fortitude may surprise everyone and be able to go on courageously.

A marvelous example of this gift is represented in the opera *The Dialogue of the Carmelites*, by Francis Poulenc. In this opera, a convent of cloistered Carmelite nuns in France learns that they are to be arrested and guillotined in the town square the next day. It is the reign of terror. The prioress, not wishing to impose death on any of the sisters, tells them that one of the doors of the convent has been left unlocked at night and if any wish to leave, they can leave. The next morning, one of the nuns, a rather fastidious and shy person, Sister Blanche, is gone. In the last scene of the opera, the sisters are marched up onto the platform to the guillotine, and one by one go to their deaths at the far end of the stage in the darkness. While they approach death, repeatedly they sing the first words of the great hymn to the Holy Spirit written by Cardinal Stephen Langdon, Archbishop of Canterbury eight hundred years ago: "*Veni Sancte Spiritus* (Come O Holy Spirit)". This beautiful hymn speaks of the gifts of the Holy Spirit, which surmount human weaknesses:

> Heal our wounds; our strength renew.
> On our dryness, pour Thy dew.
> Wash the stains of guilt away.
> Bend the stubborn heart and will.
> Melt the frozen. Warm the chill.
> Guide the steps that go astray.
> On Thy faithful who implore
> and confess Thee evermore
> in Thy sevenfold gifts descend.[1]

Among the seven gifts of the Holy Spirit is courage or fortitude. As the second to the last sister goes down to the guillotine, the prioress alone is singing *Veni Sancte Spiritus*. In one of the great moments in opera, she hears another soprano voice coming from the crowd gathered below the gallows. She turns and sees Sister Blanche coming up out of the crowd, singing *Veni Sancte Spiritus*. And the curtain goes down on this marvelous tribute to the gifts of the Holy Spirit, and the applause explodes.

---

[1] Father Caswall's translation.

CHAPTER SIX

The Meditation on the Cross of Christ

Many people have found that in times of great stress or difficulty they have been strengthened by meditating on the Passion and death of our Lord Jesus Christ and particularly, on His crucifixion. Cardinal Newman has said that meaning is given to everything in life by the crucifixion and death of Jesus Christ.

> Ten thousand things come before us one after another in the course of life and what are we to think of them? Are we to make greater things of little consequence, or least things of great consequence? How are we to look at things? This is the question which all persons of observation ask themselves and answer each in his own way. They wish to think by rule, by something within them, which may harmonize and adjust what is without them. Such is the need felt by reflective minds. Now, let me ask, what is the real key, what is the Christian interpretation of the world? What is given us by revelation to estimate and measure this world by? Crucifixion of the Son of God.
>
> It is the death of the Eternal Word of God made flesh which is our great lesson how to think and how to speak of this world. His Cross has put its due value upon everything which we see, upon all fortunes, all advantages, all ranks, the trials, the temptations, the sufferings of our earthy state.

It has brought together and made consistent all that seemed discordant and aimless. It has taught us how to live, how to use this world, what to expect, what to desire, what to hope. It is the tone into which all the strains of this world's music are ultimately to be resolved.[1]

Although persons in great distress may not feel that they can pray with much attention, they will find it easier to pray to Christ Crucified and to meditate on His sufferings because they feel a common experience with Him. It is a mysterious fact that the Passion of Christ goes on to the end of the world although our Divine Savior ceased to suffer at the ninth hour on that terrible day we call Good Friday. In His Mystical Body, that is to say, His loving embrace of those who believe in Him and His persistent calling of all those who are to be saved, He continues to suffer. The old medieval saying is that everything changes, but the cross stands firm, in place.

A person who has suffered greatly should prayerfully and meditatively read the account of the Passion in one of the Gospels. The Passion narratives begin in the following chapters: Matthew 26; Mark 14; Luke 22; and John, with the preparatory events beginning in chapter 11. We have only given brief selections for the Passion meditations in chapter 4 of this book. I find the greatest consolation in meditating on the Passion of Christ in John.

So immensely powerful are these pages of Scripture that they have been immortalized by some of the greatest music in the history of the world. Bach's different passions, especially his *Passion according to Saint Matthew* is one

---

[1] John Henry Newman, *Parochial and Plain Sermons*, book 6, Sermon 7, 2nd ed. (San Francisco: Ignatius Press, 1997), pp. 1239-45.

of the greatest masterpieces of choral music imaginable. If a person loves music, they might be listening to the Saint Matthew Passion at this time.

Steps in Meditating on the Passion

The first thing to do is to spend a little time with a picture of Christ condemned, Christ beaten, Christ crucified, in your mind. There are many artistic presentations of this, and the one on the cover of this book by an unknown, nineteenth-century artist is one that I find most moving. We can see in this painting the tears of Christ, the tears of God. Try to imagine yourself realistically there and ask yourself what the terrible calamity of the Passion meant to Jesus, His Mother and His followers.

There's something that needs to be pointed out. Devout believers have heard of the Passion and suffering of Christ so often that it almost comes to seem like a drama. The events of Holy Week reflected in the liturgy seem like predetermined dramas, at the end of which we all know there will be the glorious Resurrection. That's not how a person should pray. One should step back and put oneself very realistically in the present moment of Holy Thursday when Christ is beginning to suffer or even a few days before, as described in the Gospel of Saint John, where Christ prays that God will be glorified by His Passion and the voice from the heavens speaks to Him. It is interesting that this passage is where the Gentiles, or non-Jews, which means most of the people reading this book, come into contact with Jesus, as He is beginning to face His Passion.

One must also spend a little time in bringing the figure of the Blessed Mother of Christ into one's mind. Surely, like any true mother, she must have prayed fervently and with great distress that her Son would not be arrested, that His death He predicted would not occur. He had already said, "Behold we are going up to Jerusalem, and everything that is written of the Son of man by the prophets will be accomplished. For he will be delivered to the Gentiles, and will be mocked and shamefully treated and spit upon; they will scourge him and kill him, and on the third day he will rise" (Lk 18:31–33).

In the magnificent classic poem, given at the back of this book, the *Stabat Mater*, the author, Fra Jacapone Da Todi, has powerfully expressed what our response should be, not only to Christ, but to His Mother standing beneath the Cross.

Spend some time as you read the Gospel accounts of the Passion, asking yourself how Christ felt before Pilate, how He felt when He was scourged and beaten so much that He almost died. What did He experience as He was carrying the heavy cross beam up the side of Calvary? What were His thoughts as He was dying of asphyxiation and loss of blood on the Cross? Ask yourself the feelings, the sentiments, the pain, the dereliction that the Son of Man felt in that horrible catastrophe. You may find that, as you ask these questions, your own grief will fall into some perspective next to His. This is not to say your grief or your horror is lessened or that it is insignificant, but that it is similar, in fact because of your faith, part and parcel of His own suffering and death.

No one reading this book will have ever experienced

anything like a physical crucifixion. But some will live in great pain. Some have been through physical disasters. Others have been through terrible traumas either witnessing their dear ones in great suffering or watching as their loved ones anguish over the pain they themselves endure. Many reading this book will have lived through the tragic death of those on whom they deeply depended or those whose death, because of their tender age or the role they filled in the life of others, is a significant tragedy. There will be people reading these lines who have been humiliated by the failure of others or perhaps their own failure. There will be some reading this book who have brought upon themselves catastrophe that will scar the rest of their lives. Even these, though they may appear in many ways to have caused their own difficulties, can find some solace in the crucifixion of Christ. Had Jesus chosen to remain silent or to be more diplomatic in His encounters with His enemies and with the Romans, He would not have been there that day before Pilate. Those who have been unjustly condemned, and even those who have justly been found guilty, will find some place in which they can identify with Jesus Christ.

Some will read this book who are dying of a terminal illness; they will know that Jesus faces death with them. And in the rare circumstance that someone condemned to death, "in the death house", as they say, reads this book, he will know that Jesus Christ was there before him.

It's important to pray quietly and let the sufferings of Jesus sink deeply into your soul, and to match some aspect of the Passion with your own sufferings and sorrows. Whether your suffering be great or small, whether the catastrophe is something that will pass or a horror that has permanent effects, every one of us can sit down and say with Jesus, "I am so grateful that you are here with me."

It is the Son of God, the Eternal Word of God, a Divine person who did not, in the words of Saint Paul, "deem equality with God something to be grasped at. Rather, he emptied himself and took the form of a slave" (Phil 2:6, 7, NAB). That is the Person to whom we speak. It would seem to me that if we could move deeply into the understanding and meditation on the Passion of Christ, even the worst of sorrows or calamities would find some ray of light, some hope, in the midst of it all.

A word should be said about those who read this book while they know they are dying. Medical studies suggest that the vast majority of people dying of terminal illness know that they are dying, but no one speaks to them about it. This leaves them in isolation with what may be a terrifying thought—leaving this world. It's always best to speak about dying if you are dying. Otherwise, you find yourself isolated. But whatever the case may be, every dying person can speak to Christ who was dying over a period of several hours of incredible pain, humiliation, and sorrow. From the time that Christ was arrested until the time of His death, nearly eighteen hours elapsed, as best as one can determine from the Scriptures. Eighteen hours for a dying person can be a very long time, especially when suffering a crescendo of horrible cruelty and degradation. Christ did not die with consoling friends around Him. He did not die in bed with attendant nurses.

He died as a common criminal facing a horrible judgment. We must then see Christ in His total agony and Passion. We must enter into the sorrows of Mary. We must be there with John and even with the other apostles in their humiliation and their horror of running away. We can also even include the desperation and madness of Judas Iscariot and the grief of the holy women of Calvary who stood below the Cross.

The whole event of the Passion of Christ and His death is something modern people don't choose to think about. Years ago, the Liturgy of Good Friday presented the starkness of this event. The contemporary liturgy, responding to the squeamishness of people in the face of suffering, celebrates, in some respect, the triumph of Jesus. Personally, I have come to feel that the modern Good Friday liturgy is a letdown. It does nothing to prepare me for the crosses of life. The stark reality of the old Passion liturgy is something that I hope will be restored.

Finally, there is the end. Most people suffering bitterly cannot conceive of the end of their sufferings. It is beyond them. They cannot imagine that it will be over. Those dying of a painful terminal illness are not inclined to think of what's coming next when they're in extreme pain. A person suffering because of dear ones who are permanently damaged and humiliated does not easily foresee good things that may be coming.

For all of us, the brightness of eternal life shines beyond the darkness of death. As it says in the Preface for the Mass for the Dead, "The dissolution of this earthly home gives way to the bright promise of immortality. Life is changed and not ended." A person in the darkest reality may not be inclined to think of the Resurrection. In fact, even to bring it up to them may be annoying. And yet, it is there. The greatest thing about the Resurrection is its mystery and the fact that Christ did not come triumphantly before His enemies and walk into the Temple. Rather He was mistaken for a gardener by Mary Magdalen. He appeared along the road to Emmaus to two disciples. He is said to have been seen by five hundred on one occasion, but we have no description of this. The glories of heaven are inconceivable to men. Very few have ever experienced anything revealing our eternal destiny. A person in great sorrow may find some solace in reading the accounts of heavenly life symbolically given in the book of Revelation, chapters 21 and 22. I read these chapters very often because that's where I am going, and I await the coming of the Lord.

In the midst of grief, sorrow, catastrophe, or horror, a Christian must be waiting for the coming of the Lord. A devout Protestant woman, Julia Ward Howe, during the darkest days of the Civil War, wrote the beautiful "Battle Hymn of the Republic" about the coming of the Lord. In one of the verses she writes:

> I have seen Him in the watch-fires of a hundred
>   circling camps.
> They have builded Him an altar in the evening dews
>   and damps.
> I have read His righteous summons by the dim and
>   flaring lamps.

That marvelous hymn is a reminder in darkness that God will be coming.

Although a person cloaked in sorrow may not be prepared to think much about the divine realities at the other side, nevertheless, no meditation on the Passion should end simply at the death of Christ on the Cross, because, as the angels said to the women at the Resurrection: "Why do you seek the living among the dead? He is not here, but has risen" (Lk 24:5–6).

CHAPTER SEVEN

After Horror

Very little attention seems to be given by writers to the consequences of horror; what people do who survive and go on, and how they handle the memory of the terrible events they experienced. The most helpful efforts have been undertaken in recent years by psychologists working with what is called post-traumatic stress.

In speaking to a number of people who have gone through terrible situations, some of them lasting as long as four years in concentration camps, I have come to the conclusion that it is extremely important for survivors to integrate the experiences into their lives. They cannot simply deny that it happened. They can, if they wish, avoid speaking about it to other people in order not to relive the events, but somehow or other they must begin to integrate this experience, as impossible as that sounds, into their lives. Carefully speaking with a good counselor or compassionate and intelligent friend is, of course, a help.

I remember Bishop James Walsh of Maryknoll who had survived over twenty years in prison during his lifetime for the "crime" of being a missionary. His last stay was in a Chinese Communist prison where someone was shot every day at noontime. The victims were apparently

summoned on a random basis. Every day you faced the
possibility of death. He was in the same cell for over ten
years. Obviously, his name was not on the list.

To my astonishment, when I asked him what impris-
onment was like, he said in a very quiet and modest way:
"It was like a retreat." I then asked him how he was
treated and he said, "Not badly, considering I was a prisoner of war." He had been unable to offer Mass for over
a decade, but he had written the words of the Mass in
between the lines of newspapers that were given to him
for toilet purposes. He spiritually offered Mass every day
without being able to receive the Eucharist himself. He
smiled and said that he had concelebrated with all the
priests in the whole world every day.

Bishop Walsh, interestingly enough, refused to criticize
his captors, the Chinese Communist government. When
you would ask him about this, he would say that you
have to understand the treatment of the Chinese people
by the European powers during the early part of the century if you wanted to understand what had gone wrong
in China. Bishop Walsh happened to be the first person whom the Chinese Communist government released
from captivity.

As I mentioned, I've also known a number of priests
who were prisoners of the Nazis. Although they did not
in any way minimize or deny the horrors that they had
seen, they would often select some humorous incident to
relate, which had happened to them during their long captivity, particularly something where they had managed to

hoodwink the guards. Humor had not departed despite that horror, and, as they went on to face a new life in the freedom of the United States; they were anything but depressed people.

In the course of this volume, we've mentioned several people who have survived horror or catastrophe. The following example of survival by a creative engagement with the memory of horror is something that I think would be helpful to those living through the memory of catastrophe now.

Recently, when visiting friends, I saw a photograph of a little boy about three years old smiling at us all. I asked his mother who he was, and she told me that this little boy, her son, had died twenty years before in a tragic accident. She went on to tell me how important he was in her life, how she had come to realize that she had not lost him, that he was alive and still with her in her life. She obviously believed in an afterlife, and I did not feel it proper to ask her more questions. This youngster, now in eternity and still in her mind, participated in her life, looked after her, interceded for her with God. To her, he was very much still alive. This mother, to my knowledge, is not a formal member of any religious denomination, but obviously has faith in God and is open to religious values, including belief in an afterlife.

Unfortunately, psychologists and therapists hearing of this situation will be likely to say it is simply a touching form of denial. But as Dag Hammarskjöld remarked in his book *Markings*, "My friend the psychologist has understood nothing."[1] A very rationalistic, mechanistic point of view is not much help when you come face-to-face with absolute catastrophe. On the one hand, it is quite possible that people will deny. Some may even escape into mentally disturbed forms of denial. On the other hand, those who have lived through tragic loss, myself included, know that when one is recovering there are often inexplicable signs indicating that the deceased person is actually present. This has clearly happened to me on more than one occasion, and I have examined the experience from a psychological point of view. In some cases, it has been completely beyond any scientific or rational explanation. Someone might say, "The wish is father of the thought", and that a person in a horrible situation will desperately seek some solace and consolation in an illusion.

If you have read this book so far, I would say to you: Be careful and be realistic, but on the other hand, be open to the possibility that God, in His infinite mercy, may allow us to be mysteriously with a deceased loved one or be consoled in the greatest tragedies. The human race would not survive without hope. I reject the blanket statement that the experiences of meaning and even of blessings that come to those who have experienced horror is a form of defensive self-delusion. Not only can religious belief be the product of subjective need, but the denial of religious belief can be equally subjective. Most unbelievers I know

---

[1] Dag Hammarskjöld, *Markings*, trans. Leif Sjoberg and W. H. Auden (New York: Knopf, 1964).

have very strong motives for their unbelief, often from negative experiences of the past.

Occasionally, people who have had no religious training or belief in life after death have shared with me that, at the time of the death of relatives, they have become convinced of what they call the afterlife, that is, of eternity. Obviously, they won't have the developed ideas of eternity of those who belong to a religious faith. They certainly won't have clear ideas like Christians. The Catholic Church has not been reticent about telling people what eternal life is like based on the words of Scripture, especially the New Testament. A person without religious training will find it awkward to express their hopes and beliefs in the personal survival of those whom they love —but they may, nevertheless, strongly believe it.

When the catastrophe is not related to death, the people involved will be able to push on with hope, and even at times make things better. If you were to visit today, sixty years later, the great cities of the world that lay in ashes and ruins at the end of the Second World War, you would see proof of a universal impulse among men to right what is wrong, to restore what has been destroyed, to overcome evil with good. This impulse is placed in the human heart by God Himself.

We who believe in Divine Providence, in life after death, in salvation and resurrection; we, of all people, when faced with catastrophe, must go on with courage, faith, and hope. We must make things different. We must not remain fixed in the grief of the past, but move on to doing good and making things better in the future. The wound of sorrow will always be there. We don't want it to go away. We want the wound to heal and scar. We can work while that scar exists.

A belief in the immortality of the human soul, of the survival of the person beyond death, is one of the most important expressions of human hope. As we draw this consideration of catastrophe and horror to an end, we must recognize that hope is given to us, especially by Christ in the New Testament. He inspires this hope by His words and His actions in relation to the dead, especially Lazarus, the widow's son, and the little girl whom He called back from the dead. The meaning of Christ is most powerfully proclaimed by His own Resurrection. "I know that my Redeemer lives." These words from the book of Job (19:25) are extremely important to keep before your mind if you face catastrophe. Whether the catastrophe includes death or not, you must hold on firmly to the belief that after this earthly life, which brings sorrow to everyone, we shall be called into everlasting life where there is no mourning, no weeping, no crying anymore; because all of these things have passed away. We shall see a new heaven and a new earth and the wonderful visions given at the end of the Book of Revelation (chapters 21, 22) will be our actual fate, our destiny. How people go on without religious faith is utterly beyond me. But faith must be deep, and it must motivate a person in everyday life. Even a person who has not been trained in faith and is making the initial awkward steps toward trust in God during a catastrophe—even this person can have faith and hope. Those of us who have been gifted by God, through no merit of our own, with the Christian faith, with the vibrant belief in Christ's Resurrection and our eternal hope—those of us who have this blessing must be the best of witnesses to others who struggle with sorrow, grief, and misfortune.

Prayers and Meditations

Prayers in Times
of Grief and Sorrow

If you are a person who has experienced horror or catastrophe, may I encourage you to read and pray the selection of prayers given here, particularly the "Hymn to the Holy Spirit"? The quotations and prayers that are here will give you much to think about. The thirteen prayers involving special needs I wrote trying to express what a person would feel in such circumstances.

If you are a person who has not experienced horror or catastrophe but is helping someone who has, or are preparing yourself for a possible catastrophe in your own life and wish to face this reality that can occur any day, you would do well to read and meditate on this selection of prayers and scriptural quotations. They are not meant simply to be read. They are to be prayed and read slowly, over and over.

There is a difference between sorrow and catastrophe. I have tried to bring it out in this book. Every catastrophe or horror is sorrowful. But not every sorrow or every catastrophe is the same. Meditations on the sufferings of Christ, which are contained in the prayer section beyond this reading, will help you, I believe, to face the catastrophes that may lie in the path of any one of us. They may help you be a compassionate and helpful friend to those who are dear to you who have encountered this dark corner of life.

A Prayer in Time of Desperate Need

Heavenly Father, we know that You have provided for us all the good things that we have in our lives. You have provided for all the world and its immense numbers of peoples. I find myself today in desperate need. And Your Son has told us, "Ask and you shall receive, seek and you shall find; knock and it shall be opened to you." I do not know or understand the present, much less the future. I must put this need completely in Your hands. I know what I think I need. I know what I think the answer will be. But You and Your divine providence in Your all-knowing mind know what the answer ultimately must be. I trust in You. In my desperation, I ask You to give me Your Holy Spirit that I may continue to trust in You, that I will go ahead, that I will take the next step in the right direction. With your grace, I will endure what I have to endure: I will believe and hope through it all that You will bring good out of this for me, for those dear to me, for Your plan for the salvation of the world. I trust in You. Give me the grace to continue to trust. *Amen.*

Prayer to God Our Father in Time of Catastrophe

Heavenly Father, we know that You made life to be a blessing to us all; to be a preparation for an even greater, eternal life that You promised us. But at present I am caught in the darkest pit. An unbelievable catastrophe has occurred to me and those dear to me. I am completely confused by what has happened, and it could shake my faith and my hope.

Dear Father, send me Your Holy Spirit to strengthen me in this time of great darkness. Help me to see the possibilities of a restoration of joy at this terrible sorrow. Bring before my mind the sufferings of Christ and His glorious Resurrection.

I want to ask You why you allowed this to occur, but this is mysterious, and the question will only lead to bitterness. Help me, Holy Father, by Your Holy Spirit, to say from the depths of my heart that I trust that You will give me and those dear to me grace and courage: beyond this sorrow, that You will restore life to us, that You will give us hope now and in eternal life. I put myself completely into the hands of Jesus Crucified and Risen. His hands still carry the marks of the nails. Help me then, to pass beyond this difficulty. Help us all to return to a life where Your providence and presence is more easily seen, we pray through Christ our Lord. *Amen.*

A Prayer to Jesus in Time of Catastrophe

Lord Jesus Christ, in Your earthly life we know that You endured the worst. Having done only good in Your innocent and holy life, You were led to a terrible death. You suffered the excruciating pain of seeing Your Mother and Your friends go through that horror with You. You endured, at the same time, the cowardice and betrayal of Your apostles.

I search desperately in my own need at present to find something to hold on to, something to grasp, and I find Your Cross. O Lord Jesus Christ, by the grace of the Holy Spirit, which You send us, give me the Cross to hold on to. Give the Cross as my guide and even my light in this darkness. I don't know what the solution will be. I don't know what the answer will be, but I believe and trust that You will guide me in this darkness and that, out of it, You will bring blessings and hope. *Amen.*

A Prayer in One's Own Serious Illness

Heavenly Father, You have given me my life, with all of its hours and days and years. You have given me enough health to go on, even though at times I may have been ill and incapacitated. And now I find myself in a dangerous situation. My health may fail. My life, in fact, may be coming to its end. Sooner or later it will end. Give me Your Holy Spirit to strengthen me and especially to keep before my eyes the fact that we are all on a journey, that physical health is a passing thing, a great blessing when we have it, but it does not have to last. In fact, it cannot last forever. Give me the grace for the next day, the next hour, and help me, even in the midst of pain and suffering, to believe in Your providence and Your care. And then I will be able to find You here in my sufferings as Your divine Son found You there in His sufferings. I ask this through Christ our Lord. *Amen.*

Prayer to Jesus in Serious Illness

O Christ, my Savior, at the end of Your physical life, Your body was torn apart. You experienced extreme suffering and torture. At this time of my life, I am in great pain and

I am frightened of what lies ahead. I turn to You, as You were in the garden praying and sorrowful. I turn to You on the Cross as You were in agony, and I ask You if it is the divine will, that I may recover, that I may get back to my duties and to my life. And if it is not, I ask You to go with me to give me peace as I pass from this life to the next, to a life where there is no mourning or weeping or sorrow anymore. I trust in You. Good Shepherd, I have called upon You all my life. Now, reach out and put me into Your arms. I ask this of You, O Christ our Lord. *Amen.*

A Prayer to Our Lady in Serious Illness

Virgin and Mother of our Redeemer, you were given to us from the Cross to be our Mother. Throughout the ages, countless people have invoked you in times of illness and need. You, yourself, endured great suffering in the life of your Son and especially as His life was burning out like a bright flame. You trusted and you saw the Resurrection. I come to you, O Virgin Mary, in my sickness, and I pray for all the sick today in the whole world. I pray especially for those who do not know where to turn and who have no hope. I am grateful that I can turn to your Son and to you to intercede for me and to take my hand as I pass through this painful time. If it is God's will, may I recover and go on with my life. And if this is to be the end, help me to make it through grace, to a beautiful new beginning, which Christ has promised us. I ask this of you, O Virgin Mary and your Son, Christ our Lord. *Amen.*

A Prayer to Saint Joseph for the Very Sick

Blessed Saint Joseph, we know very little about you except that you were a righteous man and that you cared for that sacred family that was entrusted to your care. Throughout the ages, Christians have invoked you as one to implore for a happy death. It appears that Christ and Mary were with you in your last hours. I ask you, Joseph, at this severe illness in my life, to give me courage and strength, to pray for me that I may have it. And if this happens to be the time when I should leave this world, I pray that you will join me and accompany me with Christ and our Lady as I make the brief journey from this life into the next. I know that I must be purified from my sins and failings, but I trust completely in the mercy of God and that you and our Lady will pray for me and accompany me through the doors that, on this side look like gates of death, and, on the other side, are the gates of eternal life. *Amen.*

A Prayer in Time of Natural Disaster

Heavenly Father, I have lived in Your world and enjoyed it. I have enjoyed the beauty of what You have created, the sky, the land, the sea. I have enjoyed the change of seasons, the morning and the evening. And now it seems to me that the physical world has turned against me. I am overwhelmed by the destructive power that is contained in the wind and the sea and the rain, in the earth itself. It was Your providence that I should live through this earthly cataclysm, that I should suffer loss of many things, perhaps even of dear ones in this strange storm of nature. I feel betrayed by the very earth in which I live, by wind and sea and storms.

But I pray that Your Holy Spirit will give me the courage to go on, to pick up the pieces, to make a new start. It was for some reason that I was allowed to be part of this cataclysm, this disaster. Now, may I, with strength and courage given by Christ Himself through the Holy Spirit, put things back together—better than they were before. Give me the grace not to become discouraged, but to go on. And, as my earthly home may lie in ruins, may I always remember that Christ has prepared for us a heavenly home that nothing shall ever take away. *Amen.*

A Prayer in the Time of the Death of a Dear One

Lord Jesus Christ, I come to You to lament the death of someone very dear to me. How terrible and final this death would appear if I did not have hope. But You have given me hope, and You have promised that You will come and bring us to where You are. You ask us not to let our hearts be troubled or be afraid, and You promise us Your Father's home. In my desperation, in my sorrow, in my complete grief, I turn to that promise now. There is nothing else I can hold on to. How grateful I am to have faith and hope based on Your holy words, and I trust that You will lead me through this dark valley so that, again, I may meet those who are dear to me in Your Kingdom. I pray to You, O Christ, our Lord. *Amen.*

Prayer in Time of Suicide

Lord Jesus Christ, I have no place else to go but to kneel at the foot of the Cross. The death of someone so dear to me in this awful way leaves me completely confused and disoriented. It is so bitter. I am haunted by the thought that I could have done something, that I might have prevented this terrible disaster. But I don't know. I must entrust my dear one to You. There is no place else to turn. My dear one, now taken from me by the weakness of the human mind, by the inability to cope with the difficulties of life, by the wounds of mental illness, I place in Your hands. I trust completely in You that I will see those who have died this way again. I trust that, by Your precious blood and divine mercy in the last moments of life, You receive them, understanding that they have been defeated by life; and that, in no way, did they mean to go against Your will and Your law. Help us, O Lord, in this darkness to find You and to believe in Your Cross. *Amen.*

Prayer in a Time of Murder

O Lord Jesus Christ, crucified and killed as the most innocent person who ever lived, I come to You in the unbelievable and unthinkable killing of someone so dear to me, so undeserving of such a horrible crime. O Lord, help me to come to grips with what has happened even though I may never understand it. If I did not believe that You wait for us on the other side of death, I could not possibly go on. But, I believe that You, who were murdered Yourself, are mysteriously a patron of those who are unjustly killed. You are the one who leads them by Your holy Cross. I have never thought of You before with this title, patron of those unjustly killed, but that is what You are. Through the centuries, Your martyrs in the hour of death have trusted in You, and the millions of innocent people killed in so many wicked ways have, in the last moments, turned to You for hope. I entrust my dear one to You. We all know, O Lord, that this life is filled with injustice, with wickedness that comes from the evil one and from the malice of the human will gone wrong. In the midst of all this darkness, this impenetrable darkness, I turn to You with hope. Give me the grace to go on. Give me the grace to believe. Give me the grace to live life again, so that I may prepare, in the end, to find my dear ones in You. I ask this of You, O Christ our Lord. *Amen.*

Prayer in Time of Betrayal

O Lord Jesus Christ, in Your life You faced betrayal, and even the failure of Your apostles to stand by You in Your hour of need. You knew that they would fail You when they did, and You also knew that they would come back, and You prayed for them that they would strengthen us in our faith after they came back.

Lord, at this time I feel betrayed and abandoned. I turn to You for solace and hope and the willingness to go on. Please send me Your Holy Spirit to remind me that there will be better times ahead and that I will be able to understand the human weakness of those who have failed my trust. Help me, O Lord, to be forgiving of them as You forgave the apostles and all who hurt You. May the words come to the lips of my heart, "Father, forgive them for they do not know what they are doing." *Amen.*

Prayer in Times of One's Own Moral Failure

O Lord Jesus Christ, like the apostles and Judas, I have failed You, and I have failed You badly. I am ashamed, humiliated, defeated by my own weakness and inability to follow Your divine plan outlined in the Gospel. Perhaps it is because of my own negligence and lack of concern to follow You faithfully in life. Assist me, O Lord, please, in this hour of darkness. Help me to learn from my own failures, to pay the price that justice demands, and to return quietly and peacefully to a life of discipleship that may remain unrecognized by others. I pray to You, O Christ, my Lord. *Amen.*

Stabat Mater

At the cross, her station keeping,
Stood the mournful Mother weeping,
Close to Jesus to the last.

Through her heart, His sorrow sharing,
All His bitter anguish bearing,
Now at length the sword had passed.

Oh, how sad and sore distressèd
Was that Mother highly blessèd
Of the soul-begotten One!

Christ above in torment hangs,
She beneath beholds the pangs
Of her dying glorious Son.

Is there one who would not weep,
Whelmed in miseries so deep,
Christ's dear Mother to behold?

Can the human heart refrain
From partaking in her pain,
In that Mother's pain untold?

Bruised, derided, cursed, defiled,
She beheld her tender child,
All with bloody scourges rent.

For the sins of His own nation,
Saw Him hang in desolation,
Till His spirit forth He sent.

O thou Mother! Font of love,
Touch my spirit from above.
Make my heart with thine accord.

Make me feel as thou hast felt;
Make my soul to glow and melt
With the love of Christ, my Lord.

Holy Mother, pierce me through;
In my heart each wound renew
Of my Savior crucified.

Let me share with thee His pain,
Who for all our sins was slain,
Who for me in torments died.

Let me mingle tears with thee,
Mourning Him Who mourned for me,
All the days that I may live.

By the cross with thee to stay,
There with thee to weep and pray,
Is all I ask of thee to give.

Virgin of all virgins blest!
Listen to my fond request:
Let me share thy grief divine.

Let me to my latest breath,
In my body bear the death
Of that dying Son of thine.

Wounded with His every wound,
Steep my soul till it hast swooned
In His very Blood away.

Be to me, O Virgin, nigh,
Lest in flames I burn and die,
In His awful Judgment Day.

Christ, when Thou shalt call me hence,
Be Thy Mother my defense,
Be Thy cross my victory.

While my body here decays,
May my soul Thy goodness praise,
Safe in paradise with Thee. *Amen.*

℣. Pray for us, Virgin most sorrowful.
℟. That we may be made worthy of the promises
of Christ.

—Fra Jacapone Da Todi

Hymn to the Holy Spirit
(Veni Sancte Spiritus)

Come, O Holy Spirit, Thou,
From the heavenly regions now
Beams of light impart!
Come, Thou Father of the poor!
Come, Thou source of all our store!
Gladden every heart.

Thou of comforters the best;
Thou, the soul's most welcome guest;
Sweet refreshment here below;
In our labor, rest most sweet;
Grateful coolness in the heat;
Solace in the midst of woe.

O most blessed Light divine,
Shine within these hearts of thine,
And our inmost being fill!
Where thou art not, man hath naught,
Nothing good in deed or thought,
Nothing free from taint of ill.

Heal our wounds, our strength renew;
On our dryness pour the dew;
Wash the stains of guilt away;
Bend the stubborn heart and will;
Melt the frozen, warm the chill;
Guide the steps that go astray.

On the faithful who adore
And confess Thee evermore
In Thy sev'nfold gift descend;
Give them virtue's sure reward;
Give them Thy salvation, Lord;
Give them joys that never end.
Amen.

— Cardinal Stephen Langdon, Archbishop of
   Canterbury, trans. Rev. Edward Caswall

Reparation Prayer of Those
Who Have Caused Catastrophe

A notion which is not widespread but which nevertheless is very important is that Jesus, when we ask him with

confidence, repairs not only the evil we have done in ourselves, but also the evil we have done around us.

— Père Jean du Couer de Jesus d'Elbée

Dear Jesus, from the evil I have wrought around me, I ask You to draw forth good. Even I dare to ask You, draw greater good than if I had not done the evil. I ask this of You humbly, in my smallness, beating my breast and saying mea culpa, with a contrite heart, recognizing my fault. I ask it of You with immense confidence, recognizing Your mercy and the limitless price You paid for my redemption and the redemption of all whom I love and all whom I have offended.

Make reparation in me and around me. I would like to do it, but I cannot. You will do it Yourself because of my immense confidence in You.[1]

Could be most fittingly said in conjunction with Psalm 51.

Serenity Prayer

God, grant me the
SERENITY to accept the things I cannot change,
COURAGE to change the things I can and
WISDOM to know the difference—

Living one day at a time;
Enjoying one moment at a time;

[1] Pere Jean du Couer de Jesus d'Elbée, *I Believe in Love: Retreat Conferences on the Interior Life,* trans. by Marilyn Teichert and Madeleine Stebbins (Petersham, Mass., St. Bede's Publications, 1974). p. 93.

Accepting hardships
as the pathway to peace;
Taking, as He did, this sinful world
as it is, not as I would have it:
Trusting that He will make all things
right if I surrender to His will;
that I may be reasonably happy in this life
and supremely happy with Him
forever in the next. *Amen.*

— Attributed to Reinhold Niebuhr

Learning Christ

Teach me, my Lord, to be kind and gentle in all the
events of life—
in disappointments,
in the thoughtlessness of others,
in the insincerity of those I trusted,
in the unfaithfulness of those on whom I relied.

Let me put myself aside
to think of the happiness of others,
to hide my little pains and heartaches,
so that I may be the only one to suffer from them.

Teach me to profit by the suffering that comes across
my path.

Let me so use it that it may mellow me
not harden nor embitter me;

that it may make me patient, not irritable,
that it may make me broad in my forgiveness,
not narrow, haughty and overbearing.

As I go my round from one distraction to another,
let me often whisper a word of love to Thee. May
my life be lived in the supernatural, full of power for
good, and strong in the purpose of sanctity.

The Prayer of a Trusting Soul

O Lord, I offer You all of my thoughts,
words, and actions of this day.

Preserve me from selfish motives.

Grant me the wisdom, courage, and
perseverance to choose Your will over mine.
in every circumstance of this day.

Allow Your grace to flow through me,
that I might reflect Your goodness to all
whom I encounter, no matter the circumstances.

Teach me to choose God first, others second,
and myself last.

Teach me to listen much and speak little.

May I always accept Your divine providence as my
teacher and guide with all its
joys and sufferings.

May my tears always be tears of joy and my prayers always include others.

May my obedience be the measure of my trust.

May the peace of Christ guide my heart always.

Scripture Quotations That May Be Helpful for Meditation

"Let not your hearts be troubled; believe in God, believe also in me. In my Father's house are many rooms; if it were not so, would I have told you that I go to prepare a place for you? And when I go and prepare a place for you, I will come again and will take you to myself, that where I am you may be also. And you know the way where I am going." Thomas said to him, "Lord, we do not know where you are going; how can we know the way?" Jesus said to him, "I am the way, and the truth, and the life; no one comes to the Father, but by me. If you had known me, you would have known my Father also; henceforth you know him and have seen him" (Jn 14:1–7).

> Though you have made me feel many bitter
>   afflictions,
>   you will again revive me.
>   from the depths of the earth you will once more
>   raise me.
> Renew your benefits toward me,
>   and comfort me over and over.
>
>   (Ps 71:20–21, NAB)

Take courage, my children, cry to God, and he will deliver you from the power and hand of the enemy. For I have put my hope in the Everlasting to save you, and joy has come to me from the Holy One, because of the mercy which soon will come to you from your everlasting Savior. For I sent you out with sorrow and weeping, but God will give you back to me with joy and gladness for ever (Bar 4:21–23).

Truly, truly, I say to you, you will weep and lament, but the world will rejoice; you will be sorrowful, but your sorrow will turn into joy. When a woman is in labor she has sorrow, because her hour has come; but when she is delivered of the child, she no longer remembers the anguish, for joy that a child is born into the world. So you have sorrow now, but I will see you again and your hearts will rejoice, and no one will take your joy from you (Jn 16:20–22).

And I heard a loud voice from the throne saying, "Behold, the dwelling of God is with men. He will dwell with them, and they shall be his people, and God himself will be with them; he will wipe away every tear from their eyes, and death shall be no more, neither shall there be mourning nor crying nor pain any more, for the former things have passed away" (Rev 21:3–4).

> Blessed are those who mourn, for they shall be comforted (Mt 5:4).

But now, thus says the LORD, who created you, . . . and formed you. . . . "Fear not, for I have redeemed you; I have called you by name: you are mine. When you pass through the water, I will be with you; in the rivers you shall not drown. When you walk through fire, you shall not be burned; the flames shall not consume you. For I am the LORD, your God, the Holy One . . . your savior. . . . Because *you are precious in my eyes* and glorious, and because *I love you*, I give men in return for you and peoples in exchange for your life. Fear not, for *I am with you*" (Is 43:1–4, NAB; emphasis added).

"For I know well the plans I have in mind for you, says the LORD, plans for your welfare, not for woe! plans to give you a future full of hope. When you call me, when you go to pray to me, I will listen to you. When you look for me, you will find me. Yes, when you seek me with all your heart, you will find me with you, says the LORD" (Jer 29:11–14, NAB).

There is cause for rejoicing here. You may for a time have to suffer the distress of many trials; but this is so that your faith, which is more precious than the passing splendor of fire-tried gold, may by its genuineness lead to praise, glory, and honor when Jesus Christ appears. Although you have never seen him, you love him, and without seeing you now believe in him, and rejoice with inexpressible joy touched with glory because you are achieving faith's goal, your salvation (1 Pet 1:6–9, NAB).

> By waiting and by calm you shall be saved,
> in quiet and in trust your strength lies.
>
> (Is 30:15, NAB)

"Be still, and know that I am God" (Ps 46:11).

"Come to me, all who labor and are heavy laden, and I will give you rest. Take my yoke upon you and learn from me, for I am gentle and lowly in heart, and you will find rest for your soul. For my yoke is easy, and my burden light" (Mt 11:29–30).

Since you have been raised up in company with Christ, set your heart on what pertains to higher realms where Christ is seated at God's right hand. Be intent on things above rather than on things of earth (Colossians 3:1–2, NAB).

> Commit to the LORD your way,
> trust in him, and he will act.
>
> (Ps 37:5, NAB)

I can do all things in him who strengthens me (Phil 4:13).

We know that in everything God works for good with those who love him (Rom 8:28).

Do not be overcome by evil, but overcome evil with good (Rom 12:21).

But we have this treasure in earthen vessels, to show that the transcendent power belongs to God and not to us. We are afflicted in every way, but not crushed; perplexed, but not driven to despair; persecuted, but not forsaken; struck down, but not destroyed; always carrying in the body the death of Jesus, so that the life of Jesus may also be manifested in our bodies. For while we live we are always being given up to death for Jesus' sake, so that the life of Jesus may be manifested in our mortal flesh. So death is at work in us, but life in you.

Since we have the same spirit of faith as he had who wrote, "I believed, and so I spoke," we too believe, and so we speak, knowing that he who raised the Lord Jesus will raise us also with Jesus and bring us with you into his presence. For it is all for your sake, so that as grace extends to more and more people it may increase thanksgiving, to the glory of God.

So we do not lose heart. Though our outer man is wasting away, our inner man is being renewed every day. For this slight momentary affliction is preparing for us an eternal weight of glory beyond all comparison, because we look not to the things that are seen but to the things that are unseen; for the things that are seen are transient, but the things that are unseen are eternal.

For we know that if the earthly tent we live in is destroyed, we have a building from God, a house not made with hands, eternal in the heavens. Here indeed we groan, and long to put on our heavenly dwelling, so that by putting it on we may not be found naked. For while we are still in this tent, we sigh with anxiety; not that we would be unclothed, but that we would be further clothed, so that what is mortal may be swallowed up by life. He who has prepared us for this very thing is God, who has given us the Spirit as a guarantee.

So we are always of good courage; we know that while

we are at home in the body we are away from the Lord,
for we walk by faith, not by sight.

(2 Cor 4:7–5:7)

Psalm 51 (Miserere)

Have mercy on me, O God,
   according to your merciful love;
   according to your abundant mercy blot out my
      transgressions.
Wash me thoroughly from my iniquity,
   and cleanse me from my sin!
For I know my transgressions,
   and my sin is ever before me.
Against you, you only, have I sinned,
   and done that which is evil in your sight,
so that you are justified in your sentence
   and blameless in your judgment.
Behold, I was brought forth in iniquity,
   and in sin did my mother conceive me.
Behold, you desire truth in the inward being;
   therefore teach me wisdom in my secret heart.
Purge me with hyssop, and I shall be clean;
   wash me, and I shall be whiter than snow.
Make me hear joy and gladness;
   let the bones which you have broken rejoice.
Hide your face from my sins,
   and blot out all my iniquities.
Create in me a clean heart, O God,
   and put a new and right spirit within me.

Cast me not away from your presence,
   and take not your holy Spirit from me.
Restore to me the joy of your salvation,
   and uphold me with a willing spirit.
Then I will teach transgressors your ways,
   and sinners will return to you.
Deliver me from bloodguilt, O God,
   O God of my salvation,
   and my tongue will sing aloud of your deliverance.
O Lord, open my lips,
   and my mouth shall show forth your praise.
For you take no delight in sacrifice;
   were I to give a burnt offering, you would not
     be pleased.
The sacrifice acceptable to God is a broken spirit;
   a broken and contrite heart, O God, you will
     not despise.

(Psalm 51:1–17)

Additional Readings

The Agony in the Garden
Gerald Vann, O.P.

The history of mankind is a love-story. It is the story of how man was made for God, and then became estranged from God, but in the end, after many struggles and many sorrows, is to come back again to God, to be happy again in the end.

And the climax of that story begins in a garden, in Gethsemane; because it is there that begin those events we call the Passion of our Lord, the events which make it possible for us, here and now, to find our way home to God. And so those *events have a double character.* You can see them *simply as the effects of other events* in history: the effects of the hatred of the Scribes and priests, the fears of Pilate; *but on the other hand you can see them for what they are in themselves and for us:* you can see them as the struggle with the darkness, the victory of evil, the way back to life. And in that sense they are the fulfillment of all humanity's dreams: they do what the human heart has always longed, and must always long to do.

"So Jesus came . . . to a plot of land called Gethsemane." We begin with the Agony in the Garden: what has that to tell us about our own lives, our own struggle, our own sorrows and sins?

The first thing it tells us is a thing of comfort. And He prayed: "Father, if it be possible, let this chalice pass from me." It was for this, it was to drink this cup, that he had come on earth; and yet now he prays that he may not have to drink it. He prays to be released from his destiny. We sometimes think of the saints as though they lived in a world very remote from ours, as though they were free from our struggles and tensions and fears, as though they were able to give up home and friends, yes, and life too, without a struggle, without any shrinking, without any heartbreak. How wrong we are! "Father, let this chalice pass from me . . . And his sweat became as it were drops of blood. Father, if it be possible. . . ." *Whatever else holiness may mean, it cannot mean that we are expected to take every pain, every sorrow, as though it were no pain or sorrow at all.* "My soul is sorrowful even unto death. . . ."

What else does holiness mean: "Nevertheless", he goes on, "not my will but thine be done." *Holiness is not a question of what we feel; it is a question of what we will.* "*Thy* will be done." We say it so often; if we could say it without any reservations, wholeheartedly, we should be saints. A saint can fear his destiny and want to escape it; he can pray to be released from it; he can be heartbroken because of it; but because he is a saint he puts all his fears and his prayers and his sorrows into God's hands; "not my will but thine be done." And it is by doing that that he shows how much he loves God; it is because he does *that* that he becomes a perfect instrument for God's purposes, becomes filled with power, the power that can help to save and heal the world. For *the only thing that can heal the world is love.*[1]

The Tears of God
Gerald Vann, O.P.

Evil produces its ineluctable consequences, and the world is drenched in pain, but at every point in time and space where pain has its kingdom, there also are the tears of God, and sooner or later through the tears the soul of the world is renewed.[2]

The Person Who Is a "Neighbor"
Pope John Paul II

The parable of the Good Samaritan belongs to the Gospel of suffering. For it indicates what the relationship of each of us must be towards our suffering neighbor. We are not allowed to "pass by on the other side" indifferently; we must "stop" beside him. Everyone who stops beside the suffering of another person, whatever form it may take, is a Good Samaritan. This stopping does not mean curiosity but availability. It is like the opening of a certain interior disposition of the heart, which also has an emotional expression of its own. The name "Good Samari-

---

[1] Gerald Vann, O.P., *The Pain of Christ and the Sorrow of God* (New York: Alba House, 1994), pp. 1–3; emphasis added.

[2] Ibid., p. 97.

tan" fits every individual who is sensitive to the sufferings of others, who "is moved" by the misfortune of another. If Christ, who knows the interior of man, empha-
sizes this compassion, this means that it is important for
our whole attitude toward others' suffering. Therefore
one must cultivate this sensitivity of heart, which bears
witness to compassion towards a suffering person. Sometimes this compassion remains the only principal expression of our love for and solidarity with the sufferer.

Nevertheless, the Good Samaritan of Christ's parable
does not stop at sympathy and compassion alone. They
become for him an incentive to actions aimed at bringing help to the injured man. In a word, then, a Good
Samaritan is one who brings help in suffering, whatever
its nature may be. Help which is, as far as possible, effective. He puts his whole heart into it, nor does he spare
material means. We can say that he gives himself, his very
"I," opening this "I" to the other person. Here we touch
upon one of the key points of all Christian anthropology.
Man cannot "fully find himself except through a sincere
gift of himself" (*Gaudium et Spes*, 24). A Good Samaritan
is the person capable of exactly such a gift of self.

Following the parable of the Gospel, we could say that
suffering, which is present under so many different forms
in our human world, is also present in order to unleash
love in the human person, that unselfish gift of one's "I"
on behalf of other people, especially those who suffer.
The world of human suffering unceasingly calls for, so
to speak, another world: the world of human love; and in
a certain sense man owes to suffering that unselfish love

which stirs in his heart and actions. The person who is a "neighbor" cannot indifferently pass by the suffering of another: this in the name of fundamental human solidarity, still more in the name of love of neighbor. He must "stop," "sympathize," just like the Samaritan of the Gospel parable. The parable in itself expresses a deeply Christian truth, but one that at the same time is very universally human. It is not without reason that, also in ordinary speech, any activity on behalf of the suffering and needy is called "Good Samaritan" work.[3]

Suffering More Than Anything Else
Makes Present the Power of Redemption
Pope John Paul II

Faith in sharing in the suffering of Christ brings with it the interior certainty that the suffering person "completes what is lacking in Christ's afflictions"; the certainty that in the spiritual dimension of the work of Redemption he is serving, like Christ, the salvation of his brothers and sisters. Therefore, he is carrying out an irreplaceable service. In the Body of Christ, which is ceaselessly born of the cross of the Redeemer, it is precisely suffering permeated by the spirit of Christ's sacrifice that is the irreplaceable mediator and author of the good things which are indispensable for the world's salvation. *It is suffering, more than anything else, which clears the way for the grace which*

---

[3] Pope John Paul II, *Salvifici Doloris: On the Christian Meaning of Human Suffering*, nos. 28–29.

transforms human souls. Suffering, more than anything else, makes present in the history of humanity the powers of the Redemption. In that "cosmic" struggle between the spiritual powers of good and evil, spoken of in the letter to the Ephesians (6:12), *human sufferings, united to the redemptive suffering of Christ, constitute a special support for the powers of good, and open the way to the victory of these salvific powers.*[4]

Suffering Transformed from Within
Pope John Paul II

"*Christ has made suffering the firmest basis of the definitive good, namely, the good of eternal salvation. . . .*" Christ guides the suffering human soul through its interior journey alongside His own redemptive suffering on the cross but with the consolation of the Holy Spirit and in the company of the Blessed Virgin. "*[E]very form of suffering, given fresh life by the power of this cross, should become no longer the weakness of man but the power of God.*"

Though each suffering soul approaches and reacts to his or her personal cross of suffering differently, most wonder why, seeking "*an answer to this question on a human level.*"

The response comes slowly, at first imperceptibly, not as an answer at all, but as "*a call,*" "*a vocation.*" Through the soul's very human pain and anguish, Christ requests its

---

[4] Ibid., no. 27; emphasis added.

willingness to take up that particular cross, inviting it to participate in His redemptive suffering.

This *"salvific meaning of suffering descends to man's level and becomes, in a sense, the individual's personal response. It is then that man finds in his suffering interior peace and even spiritual joy."*[5]

[5] Ibid., no. 26.